6-73

VIGNETTES OF MUSIC

EDUCATION HISTORY

By Charles L. Gary

MUSIC EDUCATORS NATIONAL CONFERENCE

1201 SIXTEENTH STREET N.W. · WASHINGTON D.C., 20036

PREFACE

The twenty pieces of this booklet have all appeared in the *Music Educators Journal* between the years 1955 and 1962. They are collected here as a convenience and have been arranged in chronological fashion. This is not meant to imply that these incidents present the twenty most important events in music education between 1837 and 1927.

The purpose of the Vignettes has always been merely to highlight a personality, method, or movement in music education in the hope that history in small doses might be made palatable. Not all of the important events in history lend themselves to this approach. If those that do help the reader catch the spirit of earlier times the author's purposes have been served.

THE SEVENTH ANNUAL meeting of the Western Literary Institute and College of Professional Teachers was convened at the Sixth Street Methodist Church in Cincinnati on Friday, October seventh in the year 1837. In addition to the professional educators from western and southern states who had come together for a week to listen to the reading of papers on all types of educational subjects, the hall contained a considerable number of lay citizens. These persons had undoubtedly come to hear a report on European schools to be given by Calvin Stowe of the Lane Seminary faculty, who, with his bride the former Harriet Beecher, had spent the greater part of the past year traveling on the continent. But before they were to have this opportunity there was a committee report to be read.

Charles Beecher, another of the Reverend Lyman Beecher's children, rose to present the paper on "Vocal Music as a Branch of Common School Education" which he had prepared in collaboration with Timothy B. Mason, in accordance with the request of the Institute made at the sixth annual meeting the previous fall. Beecher stated that after examining the questions with which they had been charged, he and Mr. Mason concluded that (1) all men can learn to sing; (2) vocal music is of physical, intellectual, and moral benefit as a school subject; and (3) to bring about the introduction of music in the schools, the popular mind must be ready to recognize its desirability and teachers of the common schools must be qualified. The Institute accepted the report and Louis Harding asked for

Calvin Stowe

the floor and said, "Mr. Chairman, I would like to place a resolution before my colleagues, as follows:

"Resolved, as the settled sentiment of this convention, that the capacity for vocal music is common to mankind, and that vocal music may be employed to great advantage, as a means of discipline, of health, and of intellectual and moral advancement; and ought to be a part of the daily course of instruction in all our common schools as well as higher seminaries."

After remarks from several gentlemen, the college voted the adoption of the resolution.

Then Calvin Stowe gave his paper on the "Course of Instruction in the Common Schools of Prussia and Württemburg." The members of the Institute and the spectators present seemed interested in everything he had to tell about the highly systematized schools he had visited. Timothy Mason was both surprised and gratified when Stowe told the Institute's members that they could see music taught at Mason's Eclectic Academy of Music by the same methods he had seen used in Germany. Stowe further reinforced the report of Beecher and Mason by saying, "all children who are capable of learning to read, are capable of learning to sing, and . . . this branch of instruction can be introduced into all our common schools with the greatest advantage, not only to the comfort and discipline of the pupils, but also to their progress in their other studies."

Many of the educators and citizens seemed convinced by this double-barreled plea for music in the schools. Harriet Stowe, sitting in the back of the hall, felt proud of her brother and of her husband. She also felt that America's schools would soon be singing.

Timothy Mason, brother of Lowell Mason, was the first Professor of Music in Cincinnati's Eclectic Academy which was modeled after the Boston Academy of Music. His first Cincinnati classes in June, 1834 were taught in the vestry of the Second Presbyterian Church where Lyman Beecher was the minister. Beecher had recently come from Boston's Bowdoin Street Church where Lowell Mason was organist.

Calvin Stowe's account of his observations on European schools, later made to the Ohio legislature and other groups, was one of the most discussed educational documents of the time. The 1837 meeting of the Western Institute, coming one year before the introduction of music as a regular part of the Boston school curriculum, is a milestone in music education history.

Source: *Transactions of the Seventh Annual Meeting of the Western Literary Institute and College of Professional Teachers.* Cincinnati: James R. Allbach, 1838, p. 259.

A<small>T ELEVEN O'CLOCK</small> on the morning of January 18, 1854, the Louisville Theatre in Louisville, Kentucky was filled with school children. Mr. Tilton, manager of the theatre, came on stage and quieted the children with a gesture.

"My young friends," he began. "Today you are to be privileged to hear one of the greatest voices of our time. The Countess Rossi, or Madame Sontag as she is known by the musical world, demonstrates by giving these free concerts for American boys and girls that she desires to contribute to the musical education of our country. The Countess first sang in opera when she was no older than some of you—fifteen. When she was only seventeen Carl Maria von Weber selected her to sing the title role in his new opera, *Euryanthe*. Beethoven chose her for the soprano parts in the first performances of his great *Ninth Symphony* and his "Missa Solemnis." After her marriage to Count Rossi she gave up her professional life for that of the wife of a diplomat, and it is only because of reverses brought on by the revolution of several years ago that she has returned to singing. What good fortune for us. I am delighted to provide the hall so that you can hear Madame Henriette Sontag and her troupe."

Henriette Sontag

As Countess Rossi came on the stage her auburn blonde hair and her slender figure made her appear much younger than her forty-eight years. She began by singing Carl Eckert's "Swiss Song" and her soprano voice was clear and fresh sounding. She then sang a polka air with variations and was joined by Signor Rossi, a basso, for Fiorvanti's "Music Lesson" duet. Rossi sang a comic "Riding Song" that sent the children into gales of laughter. Then the Countess led out a little girl of eleven and introduced her as Camille Urso, the French violin prodigy. The children applauded vigorously when she had finished playing the "Last Rose of Summer." When quiet was restored, Madame Sontag explained that her accompanist, Alfred Jaell, was also a child prodigy although at twenty-one he no longer looked it. She told the children that he had also made his debut at eleven. Mr. Jaell played "Old Folks at Home."

When the concert was concluded the pupils of the Third Ward School, under the direction of William Fallen, sang "Home Sweet Home" for Madame Sontag. She was much pleased by the rendition of the song that she herself so frequently sang. Several children carried her bouquets of flowers and she blew kisses to all her young admirers.

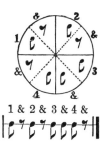

Madame Sontag gave similar concerts in Boston, New York, Cleveland, and Cincinnati. She was in Louisville on her way to Mexico City to sing for Santa Anna. While in Mexico she contracted cholera and died.

William Fallen and Luther Whiting Mason, who was also present at the Louisville concert, were the first regular music teachers employed by the Louisville Board of Education.

Sources: *Louisville Daily Journal*, Vol. XXIV, No. 46 (January 19, 1854), p. 3, "Music in the Public Schools" collected by Caroline Bourgard from the Louisville School Board Minutes. *Grove's Dictionary of Music and Musicians. The MacMillan Encyclopedia of Music.*

J UNE TWENTY-SIXTH was an unusually hot day for Cincinnati in the early summer of 1856 and the Second District schoolhouse did not offer any hope of relief to the considerable number of citizens who more than filled the largest room in the building during the late afternoon. The crowd might have been due to normal parental pride or to an interest in the new music teacher, Luther Whiting Mason. Many Cincinnatians were interested in knowing whether Mr. Mason was capable of achieving the high standard of musical results that Charles Aiken and Elisha Locke had been delivering. The children's enthusiasm for Mr. Mason may have attracted some who would not otherwise have crowded into the musical exhibition that had been announced for four o'clock.

As if to cool off their listeners the children opened the program with a song in two parts called "The Sleigh." It was a familiar tune (sung today as "Lightly Row"), but the new words by W. F. Hurlbutt and the children's singing made a big hit with the audience. The round "Come, Follow Me" was also well received. After a duet by two of the older girls, all the children sang "Don't Kill the Birds" and "Brightly Beams the Sparkling Ray." Professor Mason then said a few words about his theory of teaching music

Luther Whiting Mason

which involves the use of rote songs as a means of building a foundation for future instruction. Then the pupils sang a number of other songs including "O'er the Waters Gliding" set to a Mozart minuet, and "Star of Hope" to music from Bellini's opera, *Norma*.

Professor Mason was just about to thank the audience for coming when a girl with long, golden ringlets stepped out of the group of children and addressed him. She mentioned that his students had noticed he had never sat down while teaching them and that they thought that he must be tired. She glanced over her shoulder as she talked. "We wish you, therefore, to enjoy a little rest," she continued slowly, as if waiting for someone to come through the door to her left. Just as she began to say "It gives us great pleasure to present you with this . . ." two boys appeared in the doorway carrying a beautiful rocking chair. Mr. Mason was completely taken by surprise but not so much so as to be unable to make a pleasant little speech of acknowledgment. The children demanded that he sit down and rock in the chair, which he did. The elder Cincinnatians left the school building convinced that Luther Whiting Mason possessed an unusual ability to teach music as well as to gain the love of their children.

Luther Whiting Mason earned a reputation as an authority on music for the primary grades and as an early advocate of the rote song method of teaching while employed in the schools of Louisville, Cincinnati and Boston. He was editor of the widely used *National Music Course*, a series of charts, and a method that accompanied them. His success caused him to be called to Japan and to Germany. He was one of the founders of the music section of the National Education Association.

Source: *Cincinnati Daily Gazette*, Vol. 64, No. 312 (June 27, 1856), p. 1.

THE EIGHT HUNDRED intermediate and high school boys and girls who were gathered in Cincinnati's Mozart Hall early on the evening of December 22, 1863 were paying close attention to the instructions being given to them by their music teacher, Charles Aiken. They knew of the importance of this program they were about to sing at the Great Western Sanitary Fair, for many of them had older brothers who were at that moment in field and general hospitals which were under the inspection of the Sanitary Commission. Others were anxiously awaiting the issuance of the next hospital directory by the Commission in the hope that it might bring news of a loved one not heard from since last month's battle at Lookout Mountain. The pupils were proud to be a part of the great Fair and they hoped that their contribution would enable Cincinnati to surpass Boston and Chicago in the amount of money raised for this cause.

As Mr. Aiken finished reviewing the order of the program, the men of the orchestra began to take their places and to tune their instruments. Promptly at seven-thirty Carl Barus came on the stage and conducted the fine orchestra in *Der Freischutz* overture. When they finished, late comers filled the few vacant seats and stood at the back of the hall. Then the children rose at Mr. Aiken's signal and sang "Friends of the Cause" by

Charles Aiken

Purcell. No one in the hall could doubt that these young singers had a cause, for they all sang as if they hoped to win the war that night. A smaller chorus of students next sang "See the Conquering Hero Comes" from Handel's *Judas Maccabeus*, and then the concert singer, E. M. Powers, sang a group of tenor solos. The first part of the program included violin selections by Joseph Tosso and three choruses from the high school's music book, *The Singing School Companion*. Of these, the audience seemed to enjoy most Rossini's "God of Israel" from the opera, *Semiramide*.

After the intermission the orchestra played "Zampa" and Mr. Locke and Mr. Mason led the chorus in some selections from Part II of *The Young Singer*, the music book used in the intermediate schools. The audience demanded a repetition of "Through Helvetia's Mountain Bowers" from Bellini's opera *La Sonambula*. The high school students under Mr. Aiken's direction sang "In Good Old Colony Times" and Professor Tosso played another violin solo. Then Mr. Powers, accompanied by all eight hundred voices, sang "Stand by the Flag of the Nation." At the conclusion of this number there was a deafening roar of patriotic approval from all present. Mr. Aiken finally succeeded in obtaining quiet so that the boys and girls could conclude the program by singing "My Country 'Tis of Thee."

Sources: *The Cincinnati Daily Gazette*, Vol. 75, No. 151 (December 22, 1863), p. 1; *Harpers Weekly*, Vol. VIII, No. 367 (January 9, 1864), p. 29; *Harpers Weekly*, Vol. VIII, No. 372 (February 13, 1864), p. 98.

Charles Aiken was an outstanding figure of the early days of public school in the West. Singing school instructor, teacher in primary, intermediate and high schools, he became Cincinnati's first superintendent of music in 1871. With his Cincinnati colleagues he prepared and published *The Young Singer Parts I and II* (1860), *The Young Singer's Manual* (1866), and *The Cincinnati Music Readers* (1875). He published on his own *The High School Choralist* (1866) and *The Choralist's Companion* (1872), widely used collections of the finest choral works.

Elisha Locke, an early Cincinnati teacher from Boston, published with Solon Nourse *The School Vocalist* (1848) and *The School Melodist* (1854) both of which were used for a time in the Cincinnati schools. Locke and Charles Aiken were mainly responsible for Part II of *The Young Singer*. Luther Whiting Mason and D. H. Baldwin, later founder of the Baldwin Piano Company, were the Cincinnati music teachers who prepared most of *The Young Singer Part I*.

Lowell Mason leaned over the side of the carriage and shook the hand of his friend. "Goodbye, George," he said. "I'm glad I could visit your school and I'm always happy for an excuse to return to Massachusetts. This seems to be the best class you've had at North Reading since the war. I hope I can come again next year. Let's go, Frederick. I can't afford to miss this train." The big bay horse dug at the gravel with his hoof as if he too were worried about the lateness of the hour.

"Don't drive too fast, son," George Root told the driver. "You have plenty of time. Come back again, sir," he called as the carriage swung down the drive to the main road. The students on the steps behind him waved to the old man as long as he was in sight but he had fallen into thought almost as soon as the vehicle began moving.

A good many minutes passed before anything was said. Finally, the old man spoke up with, "Frederick, music teachers ought to be promoted

George F. Root   Lowell Mason

down." There was a pause, for young Root was not quite sure what his distinguished passenger had in mind and so thought it best to make no comment.

But now Mr. Mason felt like talking and he continued his thought after a few more moments of deliberation. "When you study and work with a subject as long as I have worked with music, Frederick, everything takes on a clearness and a simplicity that isn't apparent to you when you are young. There are undoubtedly other subjects about which this is true but music is certainly such a one. In place of new, inexperienced teachers teaching the beginners, it is these older and more competent teachers who should be introducing the subject. Therefore, my boy, I would start the new teachers in the upper grades and promote them down, a class or a grade a year, as they ripened in service."

They had arrived at the depot by this time and the younger man helped Mr. Mason with his bag. After the train had come and gone he started back to the residence which housed his father's summer school. All the way home he kept asking himself, "Did he want me to argue with him? Does he really believe that such a system could work, or was he only trying to make me think?"

George F. Root, who was associated with Lowell Mason as an early teacher of music in the Boston Schools, is best known for his sentimental songs written during the Civil War. Among them are *The Battle Cry of Freedom*, *Just Before the Battle, Mother*, and *Tramp, Tramp, Tramp, the Boys Are Marching*. His summer institutes at North Reading, Massachusetts were held during the late 1860's.

Frederick Root went on to become an eminent teacher of singing as well as an organist, lecturer, and writer on things musical.

Lowell Mason (1792-1872) was at this time of his life the honored dean of music pedagogy.

Source: *The Journal of School Music*, Vol. 1, No. 8 (1909), p. 226.

[13]

WEDNESDAY, September 19, 1877, was a holiday in Nashville, Tennessee. The schools were dismissed so that the children could join their elders in welcoming to the city Rutherford B. Hayes, President of the United States. Most of the children had to be content with finding a place along the way the President's carriage would take from the railroad station to the Capitol grounds. But 400 boys and girls from grades six, seven, and eight had a preferred position arranged up the slope of the hill on which the Capitol stands. They had been chosen to sing for the occasion and John E. Bailey, their music teacher, had worked hard with them in the few weeks that school had been in session.

These children began to get excited when they heard the Presidential train come along the river and the guns on the hill fired a salute. They were even more excited when the music of the St. Joseph Total Abstinence Band

John E. Bailey

was first heard in the distance. As the parade approached and the boys caught sight of the resplendent Standiford Guards and the famous Porter's Rifles, Mr. Bailey began to wonder if he would be able to get their attention to begin the song. Mrs. Fletcher helped him get the pitch to the boys from Hume and Fogg schools, and Mrs. Fall did the same for the children from Howard, Hynes and Belleview. As the President stepped from his carriage they began their song, "Hail Our Natal Morn." President Hayes stopped and listened for a minute and then, realizing that the crowd was growing impatient because it could not see him down behind the carriage, he moved to the steps leading up to the platform. He seemed to realize what would happen and it was as if he had tried to avoid interrupting the beautiful music that was coming from the young voices and from Mr. Bailey's heart. The end of the song was completely swallowed up in the great ovation that the crowd gave forth the minute the President appeared on the platform. The children continued to sing but John Bailey himself could not hear them as they ended their tribute to their chief executive.

Sources: *The Daily American*, Nashville, Tennessee, Sunday, September 2, 1877, p. 1. *The Daily American*, Nashville, Tennessee, Thursday, September 20, 1877, p. 2.

MAJOR SCALE.

8	c̄	Do
7	b	Si
6	ā	La
5	ḡ	Sol
4	f	Fa
3	ē	Mi
2	d̄	Re
1	c̄	Do

John E. Bailey was one of Lowell Mason's pupils who carried public school music to the South. A Civil War veteran, he taught in Lynchburg, Virginia before moving to Nashville in 1873.

During THE WINTER of 1881 the Twenty-sixth District School in the city of Cincinnati put on an entertainment for its friends. The hit of the evening proved to be seven boys about twelve years old who had been trained in a song by Walter Aiken, the music teacher. The boys sidled onto the improvised stage so that no one in the room could see what was on the large cards hanging on their backs. Mr. Aiken struck a chord on the piano and the first boy began to sing,[1]

> You may talk about your groves where you wander with your loves,
> You may talk about your moonlit waves that fall and flow,
> Something fairer far than these, I can show you if you please,
> 'Tis the charming little cupboard where the jam pots grow.

He was joined by the others to sing,

> Where the jam pots grow, where the jam pots grow,
> Where the jelly, jolly, jelly, jolly jam pots grow,
> 'Tis the dearest spot to me on the land or on the sea,
> 'Tis the charming little cupboard where the jam pots grow.

The crowd enjoyed it so much that there was a smattering of applause as a second boy commenced another verse,

> There the golden peaches shine in their syrup clear and fine
> And the raspberries are blushing with a dusty glow,
> And the cherries and the plums seen to beckon me to come
> To the charming little cupboard where the jam pots grow.

Walter H. Aiken

Source: [1]Song found in a notebook of Walter H. Aiken in a collection of his effects at the College of Music of Cincinnati.

[16]

As the boys sang the chorus this time they delighted the audience by rubbing their stomachs and rolling their eyes. Then a freckle-faced lad took a step forward and pointed his finger at Mr. Aiken in imitation of an action he must have seen in a minstrel. He sang in a clear soprano voice,

There the sprightly pickles stand with the catsup close at hand
And the marmalades and jellies in a goodly row,
And the quinces ruddy fire would an anchorite inspire
To seek the little cupboard where the jam pots grow.

As he sang the others licked their lips and wiped them with the backs of their hands just before they entered on the chorus. The biggest of the boys sang the fourth and final stanza,

Never tell me of your bowers that are full of bugs and flowers,
Never tell me of your meadows where the breezes blow,
But sing me if you will of that house beneath the hill
And the dainty little cupboard where the jam pots grow.

The voices boomed out the final chorus,

Where the jam pots grow, where the jam pots grow,
Where the jelly, jolly, jelly, jolly, jam pots grow,
'Tis the dearest spot to me on the land or on the sea,
'Tis the charming little cupboard where the jam pots grow.

Just as they finished singing the boys put their hands on their knees and in one hop turned around to present their backs to the audience. The crowd, in their enjoyment of the song, had forgotten all about the cards and were completely surprised and delighted to see them spelling out JAM POTS.

Jam Pot Song

Walter H. Aiken, with five years teaching in Middletown and Hamilton, Ohio (1874-1879), twenty-one years as a teacher in Cincinnati (1897-1900), and thirty years as superintendent of music in Cincinnati (1900-1930), presents one of the longest records of active service in the history of music education. He was a member of the Research Council of the MENC, served as host to the Conference in 1910 and 1924, and edited much music for school use.

Tuesday, September 4, 1883 was a lovely day in Evansville, Indiana. The recent rain had settled the dust in the streets and Milton Z. Tinker, school music supervisor, hummed as he started out from his home for the Canal Street School. He was beginning a full day of what promised to be a full year, his seventeenth in Evansville. On the way he passed a group of men busily engaged in erecting the towers for the new electric street lights at which people were poking so much fun. He stopped a moment to talk as several of the men were former pupils of his. As a result he was almost late for the 8:45 bell at the school building.

He spent the three hours of the morning session at Canal Street distributing the hectographed music lessons which he had compiled for the teachers to use. He felt good about the Canal Street School because Mrs. Read, the principal, saw to it that the teachers worked at the music lessons between his monthly visits and the students always did well in the individual oral examinations which he gave each spring. Then too, Julia Bierbower, who had been his assistant before the Board abolished the position six years previously, taught the seventh grade and so he could be sure that those who came to him in the eighth grade would be sight-singers and know about measure. He enjoyed his twenty minutes with the eighth grade just before lunch. They sang from "Progressive Steps No. 4" as if they had never been on vacation—that is, except for two boys who had become baritones over the summer.

He ate his lunch in the school yard and then hurried over to the Walnut Street Presbyterian Church where he served as choir director. He was anxious to see if work had begun on the installation of the new organ. R. E.

Milton Z. Tinker

Pilcher from the organ company in Louisville was directing the unpacking of the windchest. Tinker's brief chat convinced him that the Presbyterians were soon to have the noblest instrument in the city.

At the high school that afternoon he worked with three of the four classes. The juniors and seniors began to learn the "Spinning Chorus" from Wagner's *Flying Dutchman*, and the glee club rehearsed "Here in Cool Grot" by Mornington. Mr. Tinker was pleased to find over forty seniors and he felt that they would be able to sing their graduation music without help from the rest of the school. But he had decided to play safe and the juniors enjoyed the music as he knew they would. Teaching one hundred and eighty-seven boys and girls between 1:30 p.m. and 3:45 p.m. made him glad to follow his wife's suggestion to rest when he got home. He allowed himself only half an hour, however, as he wanted to study the oratorio for the evening's rehearsal. He got out his violin to help rest his voice.

On the way to Evans Hall after supper he noted that the electric light the men had been working on was burning, and that it gave almost as much light as the gas lamp in the next block. . . . The year's first rehearsal of the Philharmonic Society was encouraging although there were only seven altos. He announced the plans to cooperate with the Terre Haute Society for the production of Mendelssohn's *St. Paul*. They would sing it first in Evansville on December 12 and then again in Terre Haute a few days later. The group worked hard on the first two choruses of the oratorio.

It was a big day, as were most of Milton Tinker's days, but "associating with great music leaves one refreshed," he thought. Many of his students thought so too.

Milton Z. Tinker was born in Ashtabula County, Ohio, June 25, 1834. He studied for a short time at the Normal Musical Institute of Bradbury and Cody in Chicago in the late '50's. He had conducted singing classes and conventions in Illinois and Iowa before accepting the position at Terre Haute in 1863. He went to Evansville in 1867 and taught there until February 1914. He died in November of that year.

Sources: *Evansville Daily Journal*, September 4, 1883. *Annual Reports* of the Board of Education, Evansville Public Schools, 1881-1882.

O N THURSDAY EVENING, July 17, 1884, the board of directors of the National Education Association convened their session at five o'clock, in the Park Hotel at Madison, Wisconsin. Dr. E. E. White, who was presiding, reported that he had received a request for a new department. He said that the petition asked for the creation of a Department of Vocal Music and was signed by Theodore F. Seward of New York, Luther Whiting Mason of Boston, N. Coe Stewart of Cleveland, O. Blackman of Chicago, T. A. Brand of Madison, Henry S. Perkins of Chicago, Hosea E. Holt of Boston, O. S. Wescott of Chicago, and Daniel B. Hagar of Salem, Massachusetts. It was with particular interest that the board noted the inclusion of the name of Daniel Hagar, Head of the Salem Normal School. He had been president of the National Education Association in 1870, and was serving as chairman of a special assembly of vocal music teachers that had been called to meet during the meeting of the NEA in Madison, by L. W. Mason and T. F. Seward. Daniel B. Hagar had helped to draft the original constitution of the National Teachers Association back in 1857. If there were any in the group who should have been hesitant about admitting this new department, they withheld comment out of respect for Mr. Hagar's endorsement. One member did make the suggestion that the name be changed from Department of Vocal Music to the Department of Music Education. This was agreed upon. Then the approval of the board was given and Dr. White instructed the secretary to notify the signers of the petition of the action that had been taken.

This meeting in Madison, the result of suggestions from Theodore F. Seward and Luther Whiting Mason, was an important step in the development of the profession of music education—the broader term itself stemming from that time. Hagar was elected President of the new department, Wescott, Vice-President, and Brand, Secretary. Mason, Stewart, Blackman, and Seward, who were elected directors of the department, all held music posts in cities that hold important places in the history of music education.

Sources: *Journal of Proceedings and Addresses of the National Education Association*, 1884, Madison, Wisconsin. *Journal of Proceedings and Addresses of the National Education Association*, 1885, Saratoga Springs, New York.

J ANE BRYANT hurried toward the Second Presbyterian Church in Saratoga, New York, on the afternoon of July 14, 1892. She felt a little surprised that she actually had been bold enough to come to this National Education Association Meeting, for she was only a struggling young piano teacher. But, now that she had come, she didn't want to miss any of the first session of the Department of Music Education. She slipped into the back of the church just as President Nathan Glover of Akron, Ohio, called the meeting to order. Reverend A. H. Trick of Saratoga opened the program with a prayer. She listened with interest to a group of children from the Saratoga schools, who sang two-part arrangements of *Mount Vernon Bells*, *America*, *Tenting Tonight* and *Now the Day Is Over*. She noticed how much the children seemed to like their music teacher, David Kelsey, and how carefully they followed his direction. During President Glover's short address she glanced around the audience, predominantly men. She recognized only Hosea Holt whom she had seen many times while she was a student in Boston. Then George C. Young of Wichita, Kansas, was introduced, and

Nathan L. Glover was supervisor of music in the Akron schools for almost half a century during which time he compiled school music books, conducted institutes, and was most active in the organization of professional organizations of music teachers.

[21]

Jane noticed how fervently he seemed to read his paper entitled "The Value of Music in Public Education."

"It is almost like a sermon," she thought, "and probably better than some that have been delivered here."

When a discussion started, following the paper, Jane noticed that Mr. Holt and the others who took part seemed as engrossed and enthusiastic as men newly converted to a religion. She was particularly impressed by the remarks of Philip C. Hayden of Quincy, Illinois.

"What a long distance some of these men have come," she remarked to herself.

Then Mr. Glover was speaking again and she heard him say something about the first cellist of the Metropolitan Opera House Orchestra, who was also associate conductor of the Worcester Massachusetts Music Festival. She didn't catch the name and so, as the young man came out with his instrument, she leaned forward and asked the gentleman ahead of her. "Victor Herbert," he whispered. Mr. Herbert played Robert Schumann's *Traumerei* which Jane of course had played on the piano. She enjoyed it tremendously. This was a treat she had not counted on. Mr. Herbert announced that he would play *La Cinquantaine* of Gabriel Marie. When he had finished, Jane applauded so loudly that she wondered if she had been responsible for the

Philip C. Hayden, in addition to being a creative teacher at Quincy and at Keokuk, Iowa, was also founder of the early professional periodical, *The School Music Monthly*. He is most famous for having initiated the call to Keokuk in 1907—which resulted in the organization of the Music Supervisors National Conference (now the Music Educators National Conference).

A. J. Gantvoort was an active worker in the Music Education Department of the NEA. He was later associated with the College of Music of Cincinnati.

George C. Young served as secretary of the Music Education Department of the NEA.

man in front of her rising to offer a resolution for a formal vote of thanks to Mr. Herbert. President Glover seemed pleased at the motion and called for a vote which was obviously unanimous.

Then a Mr. A. J. Gantvoort from Piqua, Ohio, was introduced and began to speak on "Music in the Schools— What It Is, and What It Ought To Be." Jane listened for a while and then found her thoughts drifting to what she would have to do to teach in the schools. She began to wonder if it was too late to go the the Normal School this summer. Before she knew it Gantvoort was through and President Glover was reminding the group of the session the next day, which was to include a paper by Mr. Hayden ("he's good," thought Jane), a discussion led by N. Coe Stewart of Cleveland, and a lecture demonstration by Benjamin Jepson of New Haven, who would be assisted by twelve seventh grade boys from the New Haven schools, "I wouldn't miss Mr. Jepson for anything," said Jane. She knew Mr. Jepson's name for she had sung from his *Music Readers* when she was in school. This was chiefly why she had come—to see and hear some of these men. *She hadn't expected to be converted.*

Benjamin Jepson, one of the early leaders in the profession, prepared and published the *Music Reader*, which underwent several revisions. He became an institution in New Haven, Connecticut.

Jane Bryant is the author's invention.

Source: *Journal of Proceedings and Addresses of the National Education Association*, 1892, Saratoga Springs, New York, pp. 509-542.

Gustavus Junkermann, superintendent of music in the Cincinnati schools, brushed the snow from his white hair as he entered a room in Woodward High School on a wintry Saturday morning in 1896.

"I am really thankful for my Mendelssohn crop of hair this morning," he said. "You know that the great Felix patted me on the top of the head when I was a child in Germany and occasioned this luxuriant growth."

The other music teachers who were busy taking their instruments from their cases smiled at each other indulgently, for they had all heard the old man tell the anecdote many times. Junkermann got out his cello and tuned it and then called his little group together for their monthly meeting. Louis Aiken and Joseph Surdo were so engrossed in playing a violin duet that it took a rap of the bow on the music stand to get their attention. There were ten music teachers in all and several other teachers came to the rehearsals and played with the Teachers Orchestra.

"I don't want to spend too much time this morning on my supervisory details," Junkermann began. "As you know we have been asked to play for the dedication of the new Walnut Hills High School building and we need to practice as much as we can. But," and he paused for effect, "there are some things I've said to you many times before that I feel must be mentioned again. We must concentrate more on tone quality in our singing lessons. I have heard some very loud singing recently. Please, gentlemen, insist that the children sing softly and with pleasing quality. When you play your instruments with them, be careful to play softly, and will you all again ask the teachers of the very young children in your buildings to be especially

Gustavus F. Junkermann

on guard against loud singing. Remember 'Was Haenschen nicht lernt, lernt Hans nimmer.'* Now, gentlemen, let's play. Shall we begin with Meyerbeer's *Coronation March*?" "George," he said to the trombone player, "you had better move up here with Mister Rickel and Mister Robinson."

George Dasch joined the cornet players and the rehearsal began. A string on "Daddy" Zeinz's viola snapped after about eight bars and Junkermann stopped the group. The others practiced their parts while Zeinz made quick repairs and then they played through the march. They made a lot of music for the small number of players involved and Junkermann evidently thought the piece did not need further rehearsal at that time, for he began passing out a manuscript.

"This is a composition by a senior at Woodward," he said. "Walter Aiken and I think he is very talented. We thought it might be nice to play it for the graduation exercises this spring. As you see, the boy's name is Paul Ingles and he calls his composition 'Tredecim March.' Let's hear how it sounds."

The orchestra played it over and the music teachers all agreed that it was worthy of inclusion on the commencement program. Then they played through the orchestra accompaniment to Schumann's *Gypsy Life*, which the seniors from the three high schools were scheduled to sing on the same program. They concluded the rehearsal by working diligently on the overture to *Martha*.

Gustavus F. Junkermann is one of a group of German immigrants that played an important part in the 19th century history of music education. Architect, tanner, business man, school principal, before he became a music educator, Junkermann brought broad education and experience to the job. He was superintendent of music in Cincinnati from 1879 until 1900 and during that time prepared editions of the *Cincinnati Music Readers* and presented papers at the meetings of the NEA Music Education section and the Music Teachers National Association.

Sources: *65th and 67th Annual Reports of the Public Schools of Cincinnati. Joint High Schools, Commencement Program 1896. Journal of Proceedings and Addresses of the National Education Association, 1885.*
* Translation: "What the boy doesn't learn, the man never knows."

THE FIRST SERIES of papers of the 1903 meeting of the Department of Music Education of the NEA was concluded by mid-morning of July 8, and President Sterrie A. Weaver thanked C. A. Fullerton of Cedar Falls, Iowa, Julia E. Crane of Potsdam, New York, and A. Stanley Osbourne of New Paltz, New York, for their contributions. Then he introduced Samuel W. Cole, supervisor of music in Brookline, Massachusetts, and professor at the New England Conservatory of Music.

"Professor Cole and Mary MacSkimmon, who is a principal of the Pierce School in Brookline," said Mr. Weaver, "will speak to us on the subject 'The Real Purpose of Teaching Music in the Public Schools.' Contrary to the rules of etiquette we are to hear from the gentleman first. Professor Cole."

Mr. Cole began by saying that he did not believe the schools could or should attempt to teach all the children to read music at sight. This seemed to have the desired shock effect on the audience. Many of those present had come to Boston especially to see the demonstration in sight singing by President Weaver's class from Torrington, Connecticut, which was scheduled for the next day (see MEJ, September-October 1960, p. 56).

"What, then, is the purpose of teaching music in the public schools?" asked the speaker. "I answer: the creation of a musical atmosphere in America; the establishment of a musical environment in every home; the development of a national type of music; . . . In short the real purpose of teaching music in the public schools is to lay the foundation for all that we can hope or wish to realize, musically, in the United States of America. How is the teaching of music in the public schools to do all this, do you ask? I answer, first, by getting all the children to singing; and, secondly, by making the singing musical even to the point of artistic excellence. . . .

'. . . If the teachers of music in the public schools will make it their first business to get all of the children to singing, will give them the joy of participating in a musical performance, the children, when they come upon the stage of action, will support by their influence, their money, and their votes all the interests of music."

He continued his plea to the teachers present not to waste their precious few minutes on the dry bones of musical theory and rob the children of "a brief period of association with delightful music." "Some day," he continued, "if you and I do our duty, all these results in the line of individual musical intelligence will be realized in the public school, but it will be when a musical atmosphere has been created, and when those who manage the schools will see more of education in an hour of music than in an hour of struggle to find out the value of an unknown quantity—a thing which is as true now as it will be then. . . .

"To sum it all up: The real purpose of teaching music in the public schools is not to make expert sight-singers nor individual soloists. I speak from experience. I have done all these things, and I can do them again; but I have learned that, if they become an end and not a means, they hinder rather than help, because they represent only the abilities of a few. A much nobler, grander, more inspiring privilege is yours and mine: to get the great mass to singing and to make them love it. *Let us look out with joy then upon our splendid task, and, laying all personal consideration aside, build worthily and well upon the foundation which has been laid by the noble men and women who have preceded us and who have made our opportunity possible.*"

Source: *Journal of Proceedings and Addresses of the Forty-Second Annual Meeting, National Education Association* 1903, pp. 683, 695-9.

Samuel W. Cole was also a faculty member of the American Institute of Normal Methods, director of Boston's Peoples Choral Union, and a founder of the Eastern Music Supervisors Conference.

THE FINAL SESSION of the Music Department at the forty-second annual meeting of the National Education Association at the New England Conservatory in Boston on July 9, 1903 had drawn a large crowd. They had been attracted by a much publicized test in sight reading arranged by the president of the department, Sterrie A. Weaver of Westfield, Massachusetts. President Weaver, supervisor of music in Torrington, Connecticut as well as in his home town, had brought with him thirty boys and girls from a Torrington ninth grade to demonstrate their ability to read music at sight.

As the children filed in and took their seats on the stage, P. C. Hayden of Keokuk, Iowa, distributed to the audience sheets of paper which contained sixty exercises, each eight measures in length. As chairman of the committee charged with preparing the music for the test, he explained that the exercises had been written by Ralph Baldwin, Leo R. Lewis, T. L. Roberts, Harry C. Eldridge, Leonard B. Marshall, and George W. Chadwick.

"The music was printed on the *School Music Monthly* press in Keokuk and brought here by me," Mr. Hayden continued. "Thirty of the sixty items have been selected by Mr. Weaver and Miss Langdon, teacher of the class, and will now be distributed to the children."

Sterrie A. Weaver

Each child was then given a slip with the music face down. Mr. Weaver then gave a command, "Study your exercise." The boys and girls studied the music intently for approximately a minute and then, at the words "that will do," turned them down again.

At a nod from Mr. Weaver, the first two girls stood. Hazel Andrews announced the number of her exercise to the audience and gave them time to locate it on their sheet. Then she turned over her slip and sang through the eight measures with assurance. As she sat down a third girl arose and the second girl, Carrie Austin, said, "Number one." She then sang with syllables:

When she had done the first four measures without a mistake, Mr. Weaver stopped her and nodded to Pauline Bray who announced "Exercise nine."

They continued in this manner until all thirty had recited with only six of the children experiencing any difficulty with the test material. The whole

Ralph L. Baldwin

[29]

individual part of the test was finished in ten minutes, part of this time being consumed by Mr. Weaver's remarks on the value of individual work in music. Then the children sang at sight, with syllables, several four part exercises written by Leo R. Lewis. No mistakes were detected. As a final demonstration of their ability the class sang a four part song at sight with the words. All four parts were distinctly heard and Mr. Weaver, obviously proud of the group, remarked that they had not known that they would be asked to sing with the words and that the class never drilled on this activity.

The audience expressed its satisfaction with the whole test and a number of men had the opportunity to make comments. S. W. Cole of Boston expressed doubt as to the real meaning of the test since the children had known of it for six months in advance and had undoubtedly drilled hard in preparation. But the members were not swayed by his remarks and the meeting was concluded with a unanimous and enthusiastic rising vote in favor of a resolution of thanks for the "remarkable exhibition of proficiency in the sight-reading of music."

Sterrie A. Weaver established a summer school for supervisors, served as school music editor of the *Musical Courier*, and was the first president of the short-lived Society of American School Music Supervisors which he helped organize in 1899.

Following Sterrie A. Weaver's death in 1904, Ralph L. Baldwin developed his summer school into the Institute of Musical Pedagogy at Northhampton, Massachusetts. Active in the Music Teachers National Association and president of the Eastern Music Supervisors Conference (1919), he served as director of music in Hartford, Connecticut for many years.

Sources: *Journal of Proceedings and Addresses of the Forty-Second Annual Meeting, National Education Association* 1903, pp. 683-5. *School Music Monthly*, Vol. IV, No. 16 (September-October, 1903).

AT FIVE MINUTES before ten on Wednesday morning April 10, 1907, a group of men and women were gathering in the Westminister Presbyterian Church in Keokuk, Iowa. Most of them were engaged in exchanging greetings and in light conversation. Toward the front of the room, a man and a woman had their heads together over some papers. The man seemed nervous and glanced alternately at his watch and at the late comers who were entering. Finally, a few minutes past the hour, he walked to the piano and struck a chord which broke up the conversational groups. When everyone had found a seat he began to speak.

"The Music Supervisors' Conference at Keokuk is now called to order," he said. "Unfortunately, Hamlin Cogswell of Indiana, Pennsylvania, president of the Department of Music of the National Education Association, has been prevented from attending by illness. Therefore, the vice-president, Mrs. Frances E. Clark of Milwaukee, will preside in his absence. Mrs. Clark."

"Thank you, Mr. Hayden," said the lady with whom he had been conferring. "And special thanks from all of us for calling us here to Keokuk. I am, of course, honored and pleased to preside in Mr. Cogswell's stead, but I should warn you that I have just been informed of my responsibility. And now I am going to call on Dr. Ezra B. Newcomb, pastor of this church, to open our meeting with a prayer."

Following this invocation, Mrs. Clark recognized Mr. W. A. Aldrich, superintendent of schools in Keokuk, who welcomed the participants in the conference on behalf of the schools and the citizens of the town. An auditing

Frances Elliot Clark

[31]

committee was appointed and then Mrs. Clark opened a discussion on making the conference a permanent body. It was decided by a vote to delay this matter until the Friday morning meeting. Mrs. Clark then introduced Miss Alys E. Bentley of Washington, D. C. who gave the first educational address of the the program, demonstrating ways of getting young children to use their voices correctly.

* * * *

"It is now the appointed time for discussing the desirability of creating a permanent organization, " Mrs. Clark announced on Friday morning after having appointed a committee on resulutions.

A number of people were immediately on their feet with proposals. Mr. A. J. Gantvoort and Miss Anna M. Allen of Peoria were in favor of making the group a part of the N. E. A., but it was ruled that the body had no such authority. Mr. C. C. Birchard spoke in favor of an independent organization. A motion was finally made and carried that a permanent organization be formed but no agreement on plans for organization could be reached before time for a recess. When the meeting resumed, Mrs. Clark introduced T. P. Giddings of Oak Park, Illinois, who opened his talk on "The Child Voice" in a characteristic manner.

"In the good old times we hear so much about," he said, "they really seemed to know how to train voices. They had many fine singers. They

T. P. Giddings

[32]

had to be fine to get through the music they used. Nowadays, with our dramatic tendencies, if a person is able to 'holler' loud and long enough he is classed as a singer, and as such devastates his immediate vicinity. I like power as well as the next one, but it must be real, resonant power, for it pains me to hear the machinery of an overloaded voice, groaning and protesting, giving one the impression that a cylinder has run dry, or, as George Ade so aptly says: 'Her voice sounds as though she were too close to the phone.' The principal reason the old Italians . . ."

* * * *

On Friday afternoon the Girls' Glee Club from Carthage High School opened the program by singing Ferdinand Mohring's *Legends*. Then business was resumed and Herman Owen of Madison, Wisconsin, and Charlotte Field of Findlay, Ohio, were appointed members of a committee to report a form of organization. When they returned sometime later, they brought with them a constitution calling for an executive committee of nine members.

Under Mrs. Clark's direction an election of officers was held and a new organization was born.

Original officers: President, P. C. Hayden, Keokuk, Iowa; vice-president, C. H. Miller, Omaha, Nebraska; secretary, Stella Root, Springfield, Illinois; treasurer, E. B. Birge, Indianapolis, Indiana. Executive committee: Mrs. Frances E. Clark, Milwaukee, Wisconsin; Miss Jessie Clark, Wichita, Kansas; T. P. Giddings, Oak Park, Illinois; H. I. Owen, Madison, Wisconsin; Miss Birdie Alexander, Dallas, Texas.

Source: *School Music Monthly*, Vol. VIII, No. 34 (May-June, 1907).

CHARLES RICE was worried. His chorus of students from the Worcester high schools did not seem to be learning the music of Niels Gade's "The Erl King's Daughter" as rapidly as he felt they should. And the first week in October and the Golden Anniversary season of the Worcester Music Festival would soon be here. His thoughts drifted back a year to 1906 and he remembered how proud he had been of the first school chorus to sing in the Festival. They had performed Grieg's "Olav Trygvason" in a manner to make the Festival Chorus look to their laurels. How he hoped this year's group would do as well!

"They must," he told himself. "What a glorious festival it's going to be with Madame Schumann-Heink, Maud Powell, Dan Beddoe and all the other wonderful soloists." He found himself humming a fragment from one of the choruses from "Job"—the new work of Frederick Converse that had been written especially for this anniversary occasion.

He had been so preoccupied with his thoughts that he had walked within a block of Worcester's historic Mechanics Hall without realizing it. In hopes that it would ease his mind, he went over to the old structure and entered on the pretext of seeing how he would arrange his choristers. Actually, he knew the place by heart and there was little new he could do anyway because of the low balconies running along each side wall. Still, it helped to enter the half-century old building and to think about how it was tied up with the city's musical history.

"You are responsible for the country's oldest festival," he found himself saying aloud to the front wall with its tiers of organ pipes.

Then he turned abruptly and started home. The old hall had made him feel guilty about the way his boys and girls were singing. His offering in this "shrine" must not prove unworthy. He wondered if the fact that he had been so busy with the work of the Terminology Committee of the NEA's music department could mean that he didn't know his score well enough. He must hurry home and study. The students would be ready to help make this the best festival to date.

Many people thought it was.

Sources: *Musician*, Vol. 11, No. 11; Vol. 12, No. 11. *School Music Monthly*, Vol. VIII, No. 35. Raymond Morin, *Worcester Music Festival, 1858-1946*.

Charles I. Rice, supervisor of music in the schools of Worcester, Massachusetts, was a member of the original Board of Directors of the Eastern Music Supervisors Conference, now the Eastern Division of MENC. In July, 1907 at the Los Angeles meeting of the National Education Association, he led the first of seven annual discussions on music terminology conducted by the Department of Music Education. He continued as chairman of this committee throughout its significant period of service.

The 100th Worcester Music Festival was held in 1959 from October 19th through the 24th. This annual event stemmed originally from a singing school convention begun by Benjamin F. Baker and Edward Hamilton.

IT WAS A LOVELY MORNING in the old Mississippi river town of Keokuk, Iowa. On the public landing a group of boys and girls clustered around Philip C. Hayden, the local music teacher. They were all obviously in high spirits.

"You may have the run of the boat for thirty minutes," he told them, "but then, I want you to return to the main salon. Leave your instruments there. Now, let's go aboard."

At this suggestion there was a whoop of excitement and the boys and girls picked up their musical instruments and started down the steep cobble-stoned landing. The captain of the *Blackhawk* welcomed them with a blast of the whistle as they started across the gangplank. It didn't take the children long to store their instruments and to appear at various points fore and aft on the packet. Some of the boys headed for the lower deck and the engine room but the heat of the boilers soon drove them out into the open again. After one more blast of the whistle the gangplank was swung aboard and the *Blackhawk* backed out into the stream and headed up river.

Most of the children went to the top deck for the best view and Mr. Hayden joined them, sitting on a bench just in front of the wheelhouse.

P. C. Hayden

[36]

They all enjoyed the passing scenery and waved to the members of the crews of the tows that they passed going down the Mississippi. When he felt that the novelty had worn off Mr. Hayden got up from his bench and signaled to the boys and girls. They followed him down to the large room on the packet where the instruments had been left. The teacher announced that, since they had not had a chance to play together since the previous Monday afternoon, he thought that it might be wise to rehearse at least the beginnings of the numbers. After tuning up they played the opening strains of the "King Midas" overture. Mr. Hayden stopped them and they checked their tuning. Then they began an arrangement of the melodies from Victor Herbert's "The Red Mill." It went very well and after a few bars Mr. Hayden broke in to say that the only other number he wished to try at that time was the "Poet and Peasant" overture. Several children requested that they play all the way through it and so they did. Then they were dismissed to eat their box lunches and to enjoy the remainder of the boat ride.

When the packet pulled into Fort Madison the Keokuk school orchestra members were already waiting on the fore deck for the gangplank to swing into place. As soon as it settled on the bank they marched across with Philip Hayden in the lead. In a column of two's they swung up Front Street to the theater where the Lee county teachers were in session. When it was time for them to play they did so as if they wanted all the teachers to know how much they had enjoyed the boat ride.

The call sent by Philip C. Hayden to a small group of music supervisors in the Midwest resulted in the establishment of the Music Supervisors Conference (MENC). Long known for his interest in teaching music reading as well as for his editorial work with *School Music*, this incident shows that in the early teens of this century "P. C." Hayden was not unaware of the rising interest in instrumental music education.

The "germ" of this vignette came from the recollections of Edwin W. Lantz, now Director of Music in the schools of Galesburg, Illinois, and erstwhile violinist in the orchestra that took the boat ride.

A S BLANCHE EVANS waited for her first group of piano pupils to arrive in her "studio" in the passageway between the auditorium and second floor hall of Woodward High School, she discovered the December 4, 1914 issue of the Cincinnati *School Index* which she had tucked in with her music. Her eyes drifted to the article in which Director of Music Walter H. Aiken made the announcement about the institution of free piano classes.

"Maybe I need to be sure what I am about to do," she thought as she began to read.

Early in January classes will be established in Woodward High School under a competent teacher, to give instruction upon the piano. Such instruction will be free to all pupils who elect the course. For fear that the demands for membership may be greater than can be cared for by our teacher, the first chance will be given to all girls who have elected or may elect the kindergarten vocation as their career—for a knowledge of piano is part of the equipment of a trained kindergartner. The next choice will be given to those who contemplate entering the teaching profession, after which the doors are open to all. This move on the part of the educational authorities will do more to standardize the teaching of music in Cincinnati than anything ever attempted before, in the city, or even the country.

"This is a large order," she said aloud to herself. She remembered the cool reception she had encountered that morning from some of the other teachers who obviously did not approve of "piano lessons" in school and she thought back to her own school days in the Fourteenth District school when Miss Schmidt had stored her mother's piano in the room but wouldn't let the children touch it. She herself had asked for lessons on the instrument and had been denied the chance. "My own conviction about school piano classes probably stems from that experience," she mused. "It's going to take more than the flood that washed out my classes in Hamilton last year to keep me from succeeding," she vowed as she heard young voices outside the door.

"Good morning, Mrs. Evans," said the small group of girls who entered.

"Good morning, girls," she answered. "Would you each take one of these and place a chair so that you can see the piano keyboard." She passed out some models of the keyboard that she had fashioned. "First, let us find out what you know about the piano."

Mrs. Blanche E. K. Evans, one of the earliest if not the first to offer class piano instruction in the schools, died on March 15, 1961 at age 86. An MENC member for over forty years, and a Life Member since 1938, she not only taught piano at Woodward and in the elementary schools of Cincinnati but through her normal courses at the Cincinnati Conservatory of Music trained a great many of those who helped spread the class piano movement throughout the schools of the country.

Sources: *School Index* I: 14 (Dec. 4, 1914) p. 167. Interview with Mrs. Blanche E. K. Evans, August 4, 1950.

FRANK THOMPSON wasn't very happy with his situation. He had just been told that his sample cases had been held up in Omaha and could not be expected until the next morning. He thought some unkindnesses about railroads and, as an afterthought, added convention-goers, for he felt sure that all those music people that had come in with him must in some way be responsible. Since it was a fairly warm March afternoon he decided to walk back to the hotel.

"Might as well see a little of Lincoln," he said to himself.

As he walked he noticed an unusual number of automobiles chugging past him. After a few blocks he came upon a brand new 1916 White 4-45 touring car that had had tire trouble. By this time his curiosity was aroused and he stopped to talk to the driver. He discovered that practically every automobile in Lincoln, over a hundred in all, was gathering to form a motorcade to take the Music Supervisors on a sight-seeing tour of Nebraska's capital. Later, as he crossed the street to his hotel, Frank spotted the White again. It was in good running order but empty except for the driver.

"Where are your musicians?" Frank asked.

Peter Dykema

[40]

"They didn't want to go," the driver answered indignantly, ". . . said they had to rehearse some songs or something. Asked us to come back tomorrow." He clashed his gears as he drove off.

In the Lincoln *Star* later in the week Frank noted that the tour was held but that only fifty cars showed up on the second day. He was willing to bet his friend in the White was not one of them. In the same paper he saw notice of a concert by the members of the conference.

"These are certainly a serious-minded group of people," he observed to himself. "Hardware conventions are nothing like this; maybe the concert would be worth attending."

Having finished his business by the evening of March 24th, Frank Thompson decided to go to the City Auditorium for the last session of the Music Supervisors Conference. He liked good singing and had always regretted having to drop out of the Männerchor when he went on the road.

Before the program began there were several announcements that meant little to Frank. The new officers that were introduced, Peter Dykema of Madison, Wisconsin, Charles H. Miller of Lincoln, Julia Etta Crane of Potsdam, New York, and James McElroy of McKeesport, Pennsylvania, were all strangers to him. He began to realize, however, that this was really a meeting of national scope. He heard something about raising the dues and then took an interest in the fact that there were 275 associate members at this meeting, over six times the number at previous meetings. He took out

William L. Tomlins

the pass he had purchased at the box office to assure himself that he was indeed an associate member of the Music Supervisors National Conference. He found himself smiling at the idea.

Then the singing began. William L. Tomlins of Chicago was introduced as the conductor. Frank had heard his Apollo Choir years before and remembered his mother tell of Tomlin's children's chorus of over a thousand at the Columbian Exposition in 1893.

"There must be five hundred in this choir," Frank thought. He was thrilled beyond his expectations at the first number, a setting of Milton's *Ode to Music* by Parry. When this was followed by David Stanley Smith's *A Hope Carol* and *The People's Anthem* of Carl Engel, Frank decided that the practice that had infuriated the driver of the White was worthwhile, if slightly impolite. He found the whole program enjoyable but liked the chorus work better than the intermittent solos. The rendition of Mendelssohn's motet, *Judge Me O God*, he classed as his most moving religious experience of several months. Then they sang some folk songs and he had a hard time refraining from joining in *How Can I Leave Thee* and *Tenting Tonight*. He was glad when Mr. Tomlins asked the audience to stand and sing *The Star Spangled Banner*. He lifted his bathtub baritone with a will worthy of a regular member of the Conference.

Of William L. Tomlins, Edward Bailey Birge wrote (p. 155 *History of Public School Music in the United States*) "To him, at least, more than to any other person, the new emphasis upon spiritual values in music education was due."

Julia Etta Crane opened the first normal music school in the United States at Potsdam, New York in 1884. Charles Miller was Peter Dykema's successor as president of the Conference. Both served on the Educational Council and Dykema was the first editor of the *Music Supervisor's Bulletin*.

Sources: Edward Bailey Birge, *History of Public School Music in the United States*; Boston: Oliver Ditson Company, 1928. The Lincoln *Star*.

W HEN WILL EARHART, supervisor of music in the schools of Pittsburgh, Pennsylvania, approached the Kortrecht School building in Memphis, Tennessee, on a warm morning in May of 1919, he was wondering what favorable things he would be able to say in his report to the U. S. Commissioner of Education, P. P. Claxton. In his capacity as the music specialist on a team of experts selected by Mr. Claxton to survey the Memphis schools he had heard a lot of singing in the past few days in this beautiful southern city.

Mr. Earhart was disturbed by the number of monotones he found so late in the school year, by the almost universal practice of having all the boys sing the lower notes in part-songs, and by the fact that, whereas the children had much information about musical notation, it was not musically meaningful to them as reflected in their singing. He had heard a great deal of part work and some of it was commendable, but he felt sure that if he had

to write his report at that moment it would be hard for him to be very enthusiastic about the situation. He would have to be careful not to be hard on the teachers, as the spirit in the classrooms had been wonderful and most of the students were earnestly trying. He had better, thought Mr. Earhart, say something about the need for more music training for prospective teachers.

Mr. Earhart was particularly disturbed by the remark of one teacher who verbalized a prevalent attitude when she said, "We have not done much singing for two or three weeks, as we have been preparing for the music examination." It seemed that the children knew what a sharp sign did to a note but sang it wrong in actual practice. "Evidently to pass a musical examination you must first quit dealing with music," he had found himself thinking. As he went up the steps to the building he toyed with the idea of saying that Tennessee needed a musical Messiah. Maybe he would; it wasn't a bad musical reference.

When he found the eighth grade room, the class was making preparations for an operetta rehearsal. It was encouraging to note that the composition selected for this negro school production was musically good, but at the same time Mr. Earhart felt that it must present too many difficulties for this group. The colored classes he had already heard had caused him to phrase in his mind a statement that he felt covered the situation well. It would probably start off with something about the fine rhythm, the wonderful verve and

Will Earhart

[44]

abandon in singing and end with "but spontaneity reached a point where expression was more important than preliminary acquisition of the melodic line."

The pupils launched into the rehearsal and Mr. Earhart was pleasantly surprised. They sang the four-part mixed choruses with real musicianship, the basses handling the low notes with amazing ease. The solos were sung with feeling and dramatic delivery. The visitor got out his pencil and made some notes. "Lack of restraint—precision of attack—volume of tone in dramatic climaxes," he wrote. "Exceptional performance for eighth-graders anywhere," he noted, thinking of some classes in Pittsburgh. He stayed through the whole rehearsal, though he hadn't planned to do so. Lucile Washington, one of the Memphis music supervisors, came in during the rehearsal and seemed pleased to see that the distinguished visitor was witnessing the practice session.

As he left, the task of writing his report did not seem quite so onerous. He would enjoy being able to say "long, ambitious work done entirely by pupils and done well. Best school singing heard in the upper grades in Memphis."

Will Earhart, author, teacher and philosopher, taught music in Franklin, Miamisburg and Greenville, Ohio (1888-1898); served as director of music in Richmond, Indiana (1898-1912) and Pittsburgh (1912-1940); was an early president of MENC (1916), was one of the pioneer members of the Music Education Research Council; and for several terms was a member of the Editorial Board of the *Music Educators Journal*

Source: *The Public School System of Memphis, Tennessee.* U. S. Bureau of Education Bulletin, 1919, No. 50. Part 5. Washington, 1920. Government Printing Office.

W HILE GRACE BREGMANN waited for her grandson in her daughter's living room she paged through the January 1959 issue of the *Music Educators Journal* which had just arrived. On page twenty-five she happened to notice a little box with the heading "Music Educator Receives American Education Award." For some reason she read on until she came to the man's name. When she read "Joseph E. Maddy" her mind flashed back to 1927 . . . .

The "National Orchestra Train" sped along on its way to Dallas and Grace Bregmann found herself wondering what she was doing on it. Of course she knew that officially she was a chaperone of the girls in the group from Pennsylvania and that this had come about because her own daughter had been selected to be one of the thirty cello players. But she wasn't an educator and had never even been to a state PTA meeting, let alone the Department of Superintendence of the National Education Association. "I wonder what I'll find to do with myself for five days," she had said to Ann.

But once in Dallas, she never found time for that particular bit of wonderment again. She had hardly seen that the girls were settled in the homes of their hosts before she was caught up in the whirl of rehearsals and appearances. Ann insisted that she go to the Sunday afternoon vesper service at McFarlin Auditorium of Southern Methodist University to hear the strings of the National High School Orchestra play. She was so impressed with the sound of the group playing the "Pastoral Symphony" from the *Messiah* under Edgar Gordon's direction that she decided she would attend all their scheduled performances. So she was on hand Monday morning when the full

Joseph E. Maddy

orchestra of 270 players opened the program with Schubert's *March Militaire*. She was interested in the history of the cannon that Cincinnati had sent to Texas in 1836, and in the repayment that Texas was making to Cincinnati in the form of a gavel made from a tree that had been growing on the battlefield at San Jacinto. Randall J. Condon, president of the Department of Superintendence and Superintendent of the Cincinnati Schools, made a most gracious acceptance speech, she thought. She was beginning to feel as if she belonged at the conference, and she thumbed through her program for events that might interest her.

It proved to be a busy and stimulating week with many highlights. She was sorry Ann had had to miss the singing of the 600 children from Booker T. Washington High School on Tuesday evening, and she herself had been tremendously inspired by Harold Rugg's address at that general session. She hoped America's schools could become more creative. The band of 75 players from the National Orchestra led by William Norton and the twelve harpists who played on Thursday morning had the superintendents all talking about the music at the meetings. Grace had been surprised and flattered when Dr. Condon opened a conversation with her in the elevator. He seemed so pleased with the members' reaction to the music and he thanked her for her part in making the trip possible. Bringing the orchestra to Dallas had been his idea, he told her. He said something about having heard Mr. Maddy's Richmond group play in Nashville* but she didn't know exactly what he was talking about. Ann didn't either, but said that Mr. Maddy used to teach in Indiana.

*Condon spoke at the MSNC (MENC) Fifteenth Annual Meeting in Nashville, 1922.

Edgar B. Gordon

[47]

The girls were so excited on Thursday that Mrs. Bregmann made them all rest before the final program. It was a good thing she did, for even though the session started at 7:30, by the time the Dallas school children sang, and the *Rip Van Winkle* cantata was performed it was getting late. Then Superintendent Webster from Minneapolis said some wonderful things about music, but it took him too long, Grace thought. The orchestral part of the program was worth waiting for, however, and she couldn't help noticing that Ann looked lovely. Joseph Maddy had called his program "Moods in Music" and the orchestra played first Mendelssohn's *Overture* to *Midsummer Night's Dream*. From this joyful opening they proceded to the first movement of Beethoven's *Eroica* Symphony. Her neighbor commented that they played like professionals. Grace couldn't have agreed more. She was fairly bursting with pride by the time the boys and girls concluded the program with Rimsky-Korsakov's *Capriccio Espagnol*.

As she expected, the girls were too excited for sleep, but they weren't talking about the concert but about a National Orchestra Camp in the summer. She gathered it was just an idea of Mr. Maddy's but she had to promise Ann that she could go before there was any peace. "This thing does have the makings of a national institution," she thought to herself. "I'm glad I agreed to . . . ."

"Come on Grams, I'm ready. Let's get under way. Mom won't like it if we're late for her kids' concert.

Edgar B. Gordon was president of the Music Supervisors National Conference (1925-26) when the first National High School Orchestra performed at the Detroit meeting in 1926. It was he who set the stage for Mr. Maddy to organize and train this group, of which the guest conductor was Ossip Gabrilowitch, director of the Detroit Symphony Orchestra.

William Norton, then of the Flint (Michigan) Community Music Association, was later president of the North Central Music Supervisors Conference (1931-33).

The Richmond (Indiana) Orchestra was one of the first high school orchestras with complete symphony instrumentation, having been organized by Will Earhart in 1898.

Mr. Maddy, former president of the Music Educators National Conference (1936-38), founder and president of the National Music Camp, received the American Eudcation Award at the 1959 convention of the American Association of School Administrators held at Atlantic City.

Sources: *Music Supervisors Journal*, May, 1927. *Proceedings of the Sixty-Fifth Annual Meeting, National Education Association* Vol. 65, pp. 697-871.

6-302-